A History of Much Wenlock

by Vivien Bellamy

D1500775

Shropshire Books

Front cover: Wenlock Priory by Gordon Dickins
Back cover: Much Wenlock by Jim Bridgen

© Vivien Bellamy 2001

ISBN: 0-903802-79-1

Cover and book design: The Graphic Terrace
Managing Editor: Helen Sample

Published by Shropshire Books, the publishing
imprint of Shropshire County Council's
Community and Environment Services Directorate

Printed in Great Britain by Livesey Limited

About the Author

Vivien Bellamy was curator of Shrewsbury Museums between 1982 and 1994. Since then she has been awarded an MA in Architectural History from Keele University and has written articles for Traditional Homes, Period House and Country Life magazines. She is an active member of the Much Wenlock & District Society, coordinating production of the Much Wenlock Design Statement in 2000. She is now working for the Much Wenlock Windmill Trust.

Acknowledgements

The author is grateful for assistance with the text from Dr David Cox and Dr Paul Stamper, who also provided some photographs, and to Mrs Suzanne Boulos. Thanks are due for reproduction of illustrations to Jim Bridgen, Gordon Dickins, Jenny Wroe, John Muscutt (map on p iv), Bridgnorth District Council, Shropshire County Council, Much Wenlock Parish Council and Much Wenlock Town Council. Roy Penhallurick generously provided prints of his fine photographs of Benthall and Wilderhope Halls, and other photographs have been kindly lent by Mrs Boulos, Mr and Mrs E. Milner, and Mr John Morris Jones. The view of Raynalds Mansion appears by courtesy of Mr John King. Reproduction of postcards of the town is by courtesy of Penny-farthing.

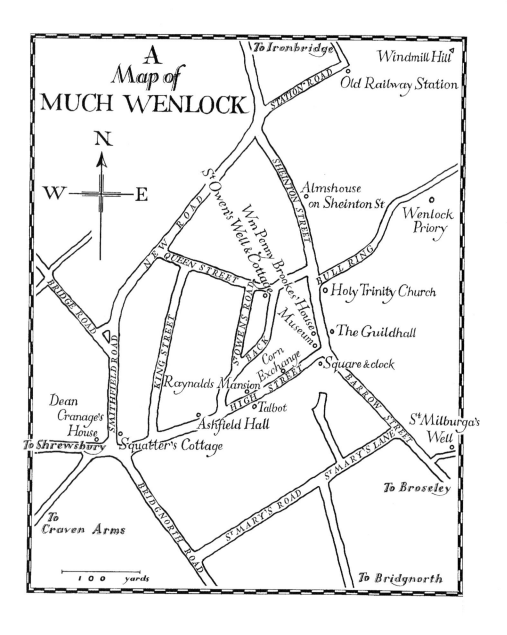

A Map of MUCH WENLOCK

N W E

To Ironbridge
Windmill Hill
STATION ROAD
Old Railway Station
SHEINTON STREET
Almshouse on Sheinton St
St Owen's Well & Cottage
Wenlock Priory
Wm Penny Brookes' House
NEW ROAD
QUEEN STREET
BULL RING
Holy Trinity Church
ST OWEN'S ROAD
Museum
The Guildhall
BRIDGE ROAD
KING STREET
BACK
Corn Exchange
HIGH STREET
Square & clock
Raynalds Mansion
Talbot
BARROW STREET
St Milburga's Well
SMITHFIELD ROAD
Dean Cranage's House
Ashfield Hall
To Shrewsbury
Squatter's Cottage
ST MARY'S LANE
To Broseley
BRIDGNORTH ROAD
ST MARY'S ROAD
To Craven Arms
To Bridgnorth

100 yards

Contents

A Much Wenlock Timeline

c.120	Wroxeter a well-established Roman town
c.450	Arrival of first Anglo-Saxon invaders
675-690	Rule of Abbess Milburga
680	Holy Trinity church founded for use of nuns and lay-women
901	Wenlock Abbey referred to in a Shrewsbury charter
1066	The Norman Conquest:
1079	Roger of Montgomery introduces French Benedictine rule to Wenlock Priory
1086	Domesday survey records holdings of Wenlock church
c.1100	Holy Trinity becomes Much Wenlock parish church
1101	Bones of St Milburga allegedly discovered
1110	Richard of Beaumais' Dictum declares all St Milburga's lands to be one parish under the jurisdiction of Wenlock
1138	King Stephen grants the Priory the right to hold a three-day fair
1163	Villeins' protest
1190	Bishop Odo visits Wenlock
1215	Magna Carta: barons force concessions from king; civil war in England
1224	Henry III grants a weekly market
1231-41	Henry III makes several visits to Wenlock
1247	Burgage system established; Wenlock known as a borough
1260	Prior Humbert makes peace with Prince Llewelyn of Wales
1267	Prior granted the right to hold markets and fairs in Madeley
1282	Start of the Hundred Years' War; death of Llewelyn and conquest of Wales by Edward I
1283	Walter of Wenlock becomes Abbot of Westminster
1284	Prior John de Tycford leaves Wenlock after defrauding the Priory
1337	Adam atte Home lends the king money
1346	Wenlock sends men to fight at Crecy
1347	First outbreak of plague in England
1379	Priory revenues diminished by effects of plague
1381	The Peasants' Revolt
1395	Wenlock Priory severs its connections with France
1421	Probable construction date of Ashfield Hall
1468	Edward IV grants Wenlock borough status in a new charter

1486-1527 Reign of Prior Richard Gosnell
1491   Wenlock has two MPs

1524   Thomas Botelar, the last Prior, becomes Vicar of
           Much Wenlock
1536   Dissolution of the Monasteries: union of England and Wales
1540   First Guildhall erected
1545   The Prior's Lodging sold as a private house
1554   Lord President of the Council of the Marches at Ashfield Hall
1577   New Guildhall erected

1600   Construction of Reynalds Mansion
1618   John Weld buys local coalfields
1631   Charter granted by Charles I
1642   Weld knighted; Charles I stays overnight in Wenlock
1645   King's rearguard troops stay overnight;
           Benthall falls to Parliament
1649   Trial and execution of Charles I; England now a republic
1682   Non-conformist preacher licensed in Wenlock

1757   New Willey Company creates iron furnace
           and railtrack to River Severn
1789   The French Revolution

1809   William Penny Brookes born
1815   Battle of Waterloo: defeat of Napoleon
1819   New almshouses built
1825   First railway opens between Stockton and Darlington
1835   Anstice becomes first Mayor; Lawley sets up printing press
1847   National School established
1850   William Penny Brookes introduces the Olympian Games
1851   The Great Exhibition
1857   Murder of Nanny Morgan
1862   Much Wenlock & Severn Valley Railway Company
           brings railway
1870-5   Agricultural depression
1889   Borough loses half of its pre-1836 area

1914   British Empire enters First World War
1917   Mary Webb publishes 'The Spring of Joy'
1935   Milnes Gaskell Family present the Linden Field to the town
1939-45   Second World War
1952   Accession of Elizabeth II
1966   Much Wenlock loses borough status;
           Telford New Town created
1992   Juan Antonio de Samaranch visits Much Wenlock and
           acknowledges its part in Olympic history

Approaches

The great limestone rampart of Wenlock Edge stretches for fifteen miles, from the Ironbridge Gorge to Craven Arms. Now protected by the National Trust, its north-western face is almost covered by ancient woodland which shields a host of natural and geological treasures. The Edge forms the watershed of the river Corve which falls gently down to Bourton in the beautiful Corve Dale. To the north, below the escarpment, lies the equally lovely Ape Dale with its sleepy villages of Harley, Hughley and Church Preen.

The Edge itself is home to several semi-magical characters. One of the more picturesque legends is that of Wild Edric, apparently an historical Saxon thane, or lord, who held Acton Scott and Hope Bowdler in 1066. He managed to retain some power after the Norman Conquest, even though he was foolhardy enough to attack the stronghold of Shrewsbury four years later. History does not record how he became reconciled to the king; perhaps it was because, allegedly, he pulled off the brilliant trick of marrying a fairy princess. If you are out late on Wenlock Edge, and lucky, you may spot this couple galloping their horses along the moonlit horizon!

Slightly below the ridge, not far from the site of the somewhat more historically valid Major's Leap, where the Royalist Thomas Smallman escaped the Parliamentarians in the Civil War, a careful searcher can find Ippikin's Rock. This is the hideaway of a legendary robber-knight, who, with his gang of bandits, preyed on passing travellers. One terrible day, so the story goes, a fall of rock buried the gang inside the cave, still counting over their ill-gotten loot. In the wake of this fearful end, various ghost stories developed. If you wish to call up Ippikin's ghost, the approved formula is to stand on the cliff at midnight and yell, "Ippikin, Ippikin, keep away with your long chin!" It is said that the apparition will appear to those bold enough to do this, but they will instantly find themselves thrown over the cliff to their deaths.

Immediately south-west of the Edge, approached from Shrewsbury
through a steeply rising cutting in the rock, lies the ancient settlement
of Much Wenlock, in a shallow bowl sheltered by rising countryside.

Historically, much of the Town's success depended on this topography,
in particular the Silurian limestone deposits of Wenlock Edge
(used for building, iron fluxing, aggregate and conversion to lime)
and its location on the western edge of the East Shropshire Coalfield,
later a source of immense wealth.

**Wenlock Edge is host to a rich variety of fossils and
wild flowers including the bright pink pyramidal orchid
(Anacamptis pyramidata) shown in this drawing by Jim
Bridgen. This charming flower is particularly partial to
limestone and can be found all along the Edge.
The paler common spotted orchid (Dachtylorhiza Fuchsii)
is found in smaller numbers.**

Shropshire is highly unusual among English counties in that its landscape
strata can demonstrate eleven out of the thirteen eras of geological time.
This rich diversity of rock forms played a key role in the development
of the academic study of geology in Britain and its subsequent
commercial exploitation. A series of country gentlemen, intelligent
and comfortably-off amateurs with the leisure for study, began to
examine this landscape with its abundant mineral and fossil deposits.
As a result, several geological features and characteristics are now
known by Shropshire names (Old Wenlockian, Long Myndian, etc).

Related to this, and an even more significant consequence, was the exploitation of the mineral wealth of the Ironbridge Gorge and its environs, including Wenlock Edge, for mining and manufacturing. Ultimately this led to the Industrial Revolution and the development of mechanised industry throughout the world.

Archaeology has demonstrated that people were living in this locality by 4,000 BC and a settlement here was probably making a living from the geology as early as the beginning of the first millennium. On Wenlock Edge, the earthwork known as Larden Ditches is probably an Iron Age fort. Walkers along the Edge can still find a whole series of quarries and limestone kilns, some of considerable antiquity. Clay for pottery was readily available and utilised from the earliest times. Neolithic and Bronze Age implements found locally suggest trade over long distances; there seems to have been a well-used route down to the river Severn. It would seem that a small Celtic community existed more or less on the site of the present town of Much Wenlock long before Roman settlement.

Just over Wenlock Edge lies the Roman city of Wroxeter, which was inhabited from the earliest days of Roman occupation right up until Saxon times. By the third century, it was well established, with a wide area of influence. Three thousand Roman coins, accompanied by a bronze brooch, apparently deposited at this period, have been found near Westwood Farm, Bourton.

Probably because of the influence of the busy city of Wroxeter, life remained heavily Romanised for local people long after the Romans themselves had left, in the fifth century. It is now clear, too, that Christianity had come to Britain long before St Augustine's mission in the fifth century. Excavation at the site of Wenlock Priory in the early 1980s indicated the existence of a large Romano-British residence, which evidently included a Christian chapel. Graves dating to the third to fifth centuries have been found near Barrow Street. All this pre-dates the Anglo-Saxon Abbey of St Milburga, whose coming may nevertheless be said to have put Wenlock 'on the map'.

An example of the expensive and highly decorated Roman pottery known as Samian ware, dating to the first or second century, was found near the present Raven Hotel in Barrow Street in 1993. (Rowley's House Museum).

However, the site may well have been selected because it was already successfully settled and lay on a well-trodden route. The development of a town here was entirely dependent on the Abbey, which had wealthy and extensive land-holdings along the Corve Dale as well as to the north, east and west. Tenants would have travelled here to pay their rents, conduct business and attend the manorial courts. Fairs and markets developed to take advantage of these regular visitors.

One such visitor was the son of William the Conqueror, Henry I, who reigned between 1100 and 1135. He is said to have built a road over the Edge at Harley Hill for his army when it rode in pursuit of the renegade Robert de Beleme, grandson of the local magnate Earl Roger of Montgomery. Henry III, whose reign (1216-1272) is notable for the establishment of a parliament, the main purpose of which was to help him raise money, came here three times. This was a turbulent period which saw the barons' rebellion, led by Simon de Montfort, in 1264, as well as an uneasy and prolonged stand-off with the Welsh, united once more by their able prince, Llewelyn ap Gruffydd. It was during this reign that Much Wenlock, a town on the edge of the disputed Welsh March, or border, acquired the status of a borough. This status allowed the town to become the administrative centre of an exceptionally large rural hinterland based on the original holdings of the Anglo-Saxon Abbey.

(Overleaf) Map showing the separate territories which made up the Borough of Wenlock.

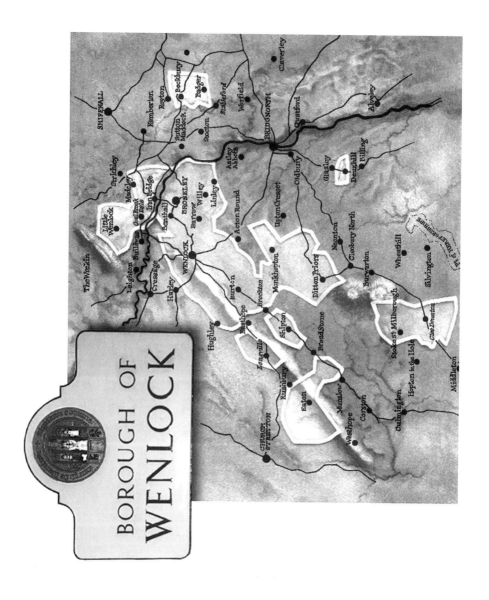

Christian Wenlock

The Priory Ruins today (Penny-farthing)

It is now understood that Christianity was spreading in Britain well before the final departure of the Romans in 410 AD and Much Wenlock's early Christian credentials have been securely established by archaeology. Legend tells of the coming of St Owen, or Ouen, whose name is remembered in a few other places in Britain and more notably in Rouen, in northern France. Coming from France, this saint is believed to have converted many to Christianity in the period after the Romans left. Christianity evidently co-existed with paganism for some time; a sculpture of a Celtic deity was found on the Priory site and various Christian holy wells in the town, including that dedicated to Owen, may be relics of earlier Celtic water cults. St Milburga's well, too, which can be found just off Barrow Street, is of ancient dedication, and the water drawn from it was believed to cure infections of the eye. It was famed in Victorian times for helping young women to find husbands.

By the Anglo-Saxon period Christianity was actively preached throughout the land and, in an age when women had greater autonomy generally, it was common practice for royal women to rule over double monasteries of both monks and nuns. These had separate accommodation and churches and, of course, extensive estates to support them economically. The best known of these examples today is the influential St Hilda of Whitby Abbey. To a woman of intelligence and ability the religious life offered a secure and fulfilling career in exchange for the many hazards of marriage and childbearing.

St Milburga's Abbey

Much of the land which was to become the property of St Milburga's Abbey in Wenlock belonged to the Anglo-Saxon ruling family of Mercia, which controlled a wide swathe of land between the Wrekin and the river Wye from their base at Tamworth. Milburga was the daughter of the Mercian king, Merewald, who converted to Christianity sometime between 670-680.

Milburga's mother, a Kentish princess, had left the king to become an abbess, a move which would not have been surprising at a time when many members of noble families chose to end their lives in religious orders. Merewald would himself have wished to assist the Church for political as well as spiritual reasons and he contrived to have his daughter running an abbey on his territory.

It is likely that Milburga was trained in the religious life and acquired some of her administrative skills at a French convent, Chelles, near Paris where many other high-born English girls, including her sister, were, as the Anglo-Saxon chronicler Bede writes, "delivered to their heavenly bridegroom". In any case, she was established as Abbess between 675 and 690 and received confirmation of her land-holdings from King Ethelred of Mercia and other secular authorities.

Evidently a very able woman, she managed to extend her estates by various means, including through gifts from devout lay people, and she is believed to have lived at least until 727. Before her death, in a document known later as the Testament of St Milburga, she listed all her territorial possessions as security against later attempts to curtail the monastery's power. After her death, legends of her miraculous deeds began to accumulate and the cult was established. She was canonised by St Theodore, Archbishop of Canterbury, and, while it was clearly expedient to exalt a royal princess in this way, Milburga seems to have been greatly loved locally.

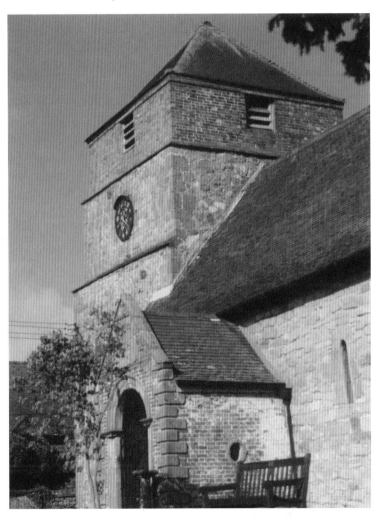

Some of the masonry of St Giles' church, Barrow, two and a half miles from Wenlock, dates from St Milburga's time, when she established an oratory, or small chapel, here.

What is now Holy Trinity parish church began life in about 680 as a church for the Abbey nuns and women of the town. Anglo-Saxon stonework is visible on the exterior of the south wall and Lady Chapel, although the present nave dates from a rebuild of about 1150. The chancel was built in the fourteenth and fifteenth centuries.

Milburga's Priory had two churches, one a rectangular building with an apse at one end in the Roman style. The remains of this, which was for the monks and laymen, lie below the present church.

Abbey Ruins

It seems that Milburga's order of nuns disappeared in time, while the monks' church developed into a minster, a church staffed by resident priests who were not monks but were expected to care for the spiritual needs of quite a widely-scattered population.

The century after the saint's death saw the expansion of Danish sea-borne power in northern Europe. During the waves of invasion by these pagan raiders Christian churches and monastic settlements were routinely plundered or destroyed. Later, however, particularly after the creation of a recognised Danish sector in northern Britain, the Danelaw, England saw more peaceful co-existence between the two racial groups and there is no evidence of damage to the Christian community in Wenlock. By 855 there were groups of Danes operating in Shropshire, and Wenlock Abbey was still flourishing at the beginning of the tenth century, when Christianity was more firmly established in Britain.

In 901 Wenlock Abbey is referred to in a charter granting it land and a gold chalice in honour of Abbess Milburga. Because women often played prominent roles in Anglo-Saxon life, it is interesting that some of the witnesses to this charter are women, even though the old abbey hierarchy, led by a royal nun, had by this time collapsed.

Whatever residual foundation existed here was given a new lease of life by the Saxon Earl Leofric of Mercia and his wife, Lady Godiva. Towards the middle of the eleventh century this couple made a series of lavish endowments which included a new minster church.

An early twentieth century imaginative reconstruction by Arthur Henderson of St Milburga's Abbey seven hundred years earlier. (Suzanne Boulos)

Norman Rule and the Benedictine Priory

Substantial Norman influence in England long preceded the Conquest itself. King Edward the Confessor was himself half Norman and had spent most of his life at the Norman court so continental influence would have been pervasive, at least at Court. The king surrounded himself with advisers from across the Channel, many of them priests and monks, who at that time were the best-educated and most literate members of any community.

Although Wenlock does not appear as an independent
settlement in the Domesday Book, as this extract shows,
the church is recorded as holding thirteen manors,
or estates, and land in Shrewsbury.

However, there were also other influences active in the Saxon King Harold's England, not least those from the Danish territories to the north. It was William the Conqueror's achievement to obliterate all these and, in the three-year campaign after his coronation in 1066, to impose French customs and French landlords everywhere except Northumbria. Tens of thousands of manors, or estates, were taken from the English owners and handed over as rewards to William's faithful henchmen. This transfer of power was backed up by the extraordinary administrative machine that created the Domesday Book.

In religious matters, as early as the seventh century a more centralised form of monasticism than that of the Saxon abbeys was sweeping through Europe, pioneered by the powerful reformer St Benedict. England's first archbishop, St Augustine, was a Benedictine and, following the foundation of the important abbey at Cluny in north-east France in 910, the Benedictine Rule came to prevail in England as on the continent.

Soon after the Conquest, the powerful Norman earl, Roger of Montgomery, took control of Shropshire. Like other noblemen, he was keen to demonstrate his piety and clearly saw Wenlock as a more important religious site than Shrewsbury, preferring first to reorganise the church here as a Benedictine priory affiliated to the French monastery at Cluny. French monks began to arrive in 1079 and over a period of years constructed the cloisters, chapter house, dormitory, and refectory which were part of the pattern common to all Benedictine houses across Europe. History records a series of French names at the Priory; this was a time when assumptions and attitudes were far more European and this French affiliation persisted at Much Wenlock for three hundred years.

Earl Roger's original priory church was re-built during the first half of the fourteenth century and, at 107 metres long, was the largest monastic building in Shropshire. The tall square building, of the same date, which visitors pass on their right as they walk to the modern entrance to the Priory, is all that remains of the original wall between the monastic enclosure and the town. At that period the entrance was at the opposite end of the enclosure from today.

(Opposite) Arcading at Wenlock Priory. There were forty monks here in the late thirteenth century, probably a larger number than anywhere else in the county. One of them, Walter of Wenlock, rose to become Abbot of Westminster between 1283 and 1307.

The timber-framed section of Ashfield Hall. On this site stood St John's Hospital. The term hospital does not imply any medical function, its meaning being closer to the modern hostel.

It was the religious orders which, in the middle ages, provided such social services as existed. In 1267 St John's Hospital, run by monks, offered accommodation to "lost and naked beggars". Like other such institutions for the very poor, it was probably sited on the edge of the town and, in view of the fact that the top of what is now the High Street became known in 1316 as Spittle (Hospital) Street, it may have stood on the site of Ashfield Hall. A stream, aptly known in 1321, well before any attempt at proper sewage control, as Schittebrok, ran through the town past this point. Later culverted, it still runs below street level.

Private benevolence did also exist, however, and during the 1480s Hugh Wolmer, a leading figure in the town, was maintaining Much Wenlock's four almshouses on the edge of the churchyard. In return, the inhabitants were expected to pray for the souls of himself and his family after their deaths.

The Shrine of St Milburga

Earl Roger confirmed the new priory in its possession of all the lands under Milburga's control. All the monks needed now, to give them the ultimate religious prestige, and the economic advantages of becoming a pilgrimage site, was the saint's body or at least some material relic.

An intriguing tale is told by Odo, a former Cluniac monk, now promoted to bishop, who visited Wenlock in 1190. He recalls how a silver casket, thought to have contained Milburga's body, was opened and found to be empty, but that, later, in a box discovered in the ruins of what is now the parish church, a Saxon document was found, recording the burial of the saint's body near the altar of that church. The monks hurried to excavate the ground near this altar, without success. But, one summer night in 1101, an extraordinary incident occurred. Two boys who had been playing in the ruins suddenly fell through the collapsing church floor into a pit. Here lay the saint's bones, described by Odo as "beautiful and luminous", accompanied by a delightful fragrance such as is believed to accompany saintly remains. This story, however, is not authenticated and doubt is cast on it by reports that Milburga's remains were known to be in Much Wenlock in 1031.

Whatever the real truth, immense economic advantages as well as prestige ensued. Because the relics of saints were regarded as conferring huge spiritual benefits, the Priory of Much Wenlock could now promote itself as a destination for pilgrimage. That this was a source of envy to the monks of Shrewsbury is evidenced by the fact that they had to resort to some very dubious manoeuvres to gain relics of their own! This tale is re-told by the novelist Ellis Peters, or Edith Pargeter, in 'A Morbid Taste for Bones', one of the series based on the fictional detective, Brother Cadfael.

Publicity, too, was an important requirement. The monk Goscelin, already famous for devoting his life to satisfying the demand for tales of the saints, was invited to stay at the Abbey sometime before 1100. In his 'Life of St Milburga', he published her remarkable Testament, referred to earlier. Although the original has disappeared, the document is considered to be authentic; in it the prudent Abbess records her substantial landholdings for posterity.

These landholdings were later confirmed by the Bishop of London, Richard of Beaumais, evidently a benefactor of the monastery, in his Dictum of 1110. This document, which stated that these lands formed the parish of Much Wenlock, became the basis for the very large territories held by the later Borough.

Prior Humbert 1221-1261

For forty years from 1221, the Priory was led by an able and dedicated churchman who was fortunate enough to enjoy the trust and friendship of the deeply religious King Henry III. Like other clerics of the period, Humbert played an important role in political life. He was entrusted by the king with diplomatic missions overseas and he also played a part in the difficult and complex negotiations with the princes of Wales. He it was who made the truce with the last prince, Llewelyn, in 1260.

Incessant noise, dust and inconvenience is not our usual modern picture of monastic life. However, these must have been the conditions at Wenlock Priory for much of Humbert's period in office. He was determined to protect the status and fabric of his monastery and, after the addition of the church and chapels of Clun to his holdings, he was granted a sum of money from the Bishop of Hereford for the maintenance of St Milburga's church. He undertook a major construction project, creating a new church and re-building the cloister. The king ordered that timber from the royal forests should be allocated to this project, including fifteen oaks for the church, four for the Lady Chapel and six for what was probably the clock tower. All this heavy labour went on, in the absence of modern construction tools, for many long years.

Nor were relations with the townspeople entirely harmonious; Humbert was accused of taxing widows and heirs extortionately and imposing an unjust tax on beer!

Between 1231-41 the king stayed several times at the Priory and accommodating his large and demanding retinue would have been quite an administrative nightmare. The Priory would have had to find room for the needs of a variety of servants, ranging from cooks, grooms and blacksmiths to musicians, and including clerks and civil servants for the secretarial and legal work. Monastic life clearly had its jolly side and minstrels were employed to entertain one grand visitor, the Abbot of Westminster, in 1290. Wine for all these guests came from Bristol, purchased for the monastery by the sheriff of Shropshire. A record exists of an order in 1245 for four tuns (barrels) for Wenlock to be placed "safely in the cellars there against the king's arrival as he proposes shortly to come to those parts, God willing." So important was this aspect of hospitality that there was actually a royal keeper of the wines employed at Wenlock.

The Priory Expands

The paramount importance of religion in every aspect of life during the medieval period cannot be over-stressed. Much Wenlock would not have existed without the Priory, which provided a social infrastructure and livelihoods for most local people. The town prospered only as the Priory did.

In addition to the prestige and economic power emanating from the Priory, Much Wenlock had its own parish church, Holy Trinity, which itself controlled outlying parishes and benefited from the tithe system, by which each area supplied a tenth of its output to the mother church. By 1274, for example, the inhabitants of Monkhopton and Weston had to supply the Vicar of Much Wenlock with both corn and cash annually as "shrift corn" for the privilege of confessing their sins to him!

The present Holy Trinity became the parish church of Much Wenlock around 1100 when a new church, described as a minster, was constructed north-east of it for the use of the Priory. (Penny-farthing)

During the twelfth century, through aristocratic patrons who had land-holdings there, Wenlock Priory briefly established a daughter house in Dudley, on the Isle of Wight. Through a member of the locally important FitzAlan family who was a friend of King David of Scotland, another was set up at the Scottish town of Paisley. More locally, there was a small priory at Preen. The monastery acquired further land of its own and was involved in both agriculture and industrial operations such as mills and iron-founding. Dozens of local men were employed by these early industrial concerns. It is likely that the nearby town of Madeley was established by the monks of Wenlock before 1269, when the Prior was granted the right to hold markets and fairs there.

Relations with the French monastery continued to be close and in 1198 the new prior came direct from La Charité. However, in 1276, visiting auditors from La Charité had to file devastating criticisms of the current Prior, John de Tycford, for financial double-dealing and fraud. In spite of this, he seems to have retained his post. Clearly a smart operator, in 1284 he managed to sell the wool yields for the next seven years and disappear with the cash!

These were lawless times; apart from what we would call the white-collar crime of fraud, there are several examples of violent behaviour among these men, apparently vowed to peaceful service of the Christian God. One scandal concerns a wild young monk, William Broseley, who surrounded himself with a band of armed men and led the life of a bandit until his final capture. A taste for violent robbery also affected some of those higher up the scale. A prior, Henry de Bonvillars, was accused of banditry in 1302. He was accused, firstly by a local landowner of raiding and robbing a farm and, secondly, by the powerful marcher lord, Roger Mortimer of Chirk, of stealing some of his breeding mares, a serious offence at a time when these would have been extremely valuable.

In the meantime, England was becoming increasingly hostile to France and the Priory, along with other institutions affiliated to Cluny, began to be seen as alien. 1337 saw the beginning of the protracted religious conflict across Europe which came to be known as the Hundred Years' War, and England became more and more isolated from the continent. The Great Schism in the Christian church, whereby two popes reigned simultaneously, one at Avignon in France and one in Rome, tore Europe apart. England maintained allegiance to Rome and, as France was now an opponent, it became politically necessary for ties with that country to be severed and for the Priory to have an Englishman as Prior. In 1395, the annual contribution of a hundred shillings, made by Wenlock Priory to La Charité, was finally transferred to the coffers of the English king.

Life during the latter part of the middle ages must have been grim, especially for the poor. Towards the end of the fourteenth century history records a series of miseries and misfortunes. After crop failures and a devastating outbreak of disease among livestock, the horrors of the bubonic plague began to take their toll. As many as half the clergy in the deanery of Wenlock died. The loss of manpower generally is reflected in the fact that rents fell to less than a quarter of their previous rate in the final years of the fourteenth century. In 1379 Prior Roger Wyvill drew up a financial statement showing a large deficit caused, he stated, by the effects of the Great Pestilence. However, the continuing high status of the parish is indicated by the fact that, by 1404, a schoolmaster was employed and schoolboys sang at church services.

At the end of the fifteenth century the Prior was a local man, Richard Singer, connected by marriage to the important More family. His reign (1486-1521) is marked by a spate of building and improvement projects. In 1504, expenditure on ecclesiastical vestments alone reached the astronomical sum, for the time, of £40. The Prior who followed Singer, Richard Gosnell, was an ambitious man who aroused great antagonism locally. But the winds of change were already blowing through the religious institutions. Criticisms of Gosnell's regime, alleging misconduct of various kinds among the monastic community, led to a major enquiry, and in 1527 Gosnell was forced to resign his position to the final Prior, John Bayley.

The fifteenth century saw substantial improvements, not least in the further development of an L-shaped extension to form an infirmary and Prior's lodging. The roof of this beautiful building, parts of which are substantially older, has been dated by tree-ring analysis to 1423. When Henry VIII dissolved the monasteries in 1540 it became a private house and in recent years has been magnificently restored by its present owners. It is regarded as one of the finest examples of domestic architecture of its period in England. (Suzanne Boulos)

In spite of these goings-on at the Priory, in the years leading up to the Reformation the vicars of Holy Trinity parish church were generally, unlike in many other districts, conscientious workers and men of considerable learning.

The Dissolution and Religious Dissent

Just over ten years after Gosnell's resignation, parish records began to be kept, at the instigation of King Henry VIII's minister, Thomas Cromwell. In Much Wenlock Thomas Botelar, or Butler, was the last Abbot and he became Vicar in 1524. He is particularly remembered because, in addition to the official records, he maintained a fascinating private journal. In this he records, among other events, that "the bones of the blessed Milburga... were burnt at the churchyard entrance". In the new climate of protestant opinion these were felt to be the object of idolatry. Twelve years later, recorded in the old parish register, are the following words: "Note that upon the 26 day of June was service first celebrated in the Englyssh tonge, anno primo Elizabethae, 1559."

Henry VIII's break with the Pope (who would not agree to the annulment of Henry's first marriage) ushered in a period of immense social change brought about largely by the decision to close down all the monastic houses and confiscate their wealth. While some monastic houses were already in decline, both spiritually and materially, sudden and catastrophic decay befell many ancient buildings which were stripped of their protective lead roofs. A great deal of what we would now consider vandalism took place. Side altars, such as may be seen in Roman Catholic churches today, were abolished, statues were destroyed and plate was confiscated. Furthermore, as the historian Norman Davies writes, "The Act for the Dissolution of the Monasteries abolished a few nests of corruption together with the greatest network of social and educational welfare that England had ever known."

An orgy of asset-stripping on behalf of King Henry, which must have horrified the devout, then ensued and all valuables were sent to the Tower of London. The great bells, which had been cast by a monk-craftsman of extraordinary versatility, William Corvehill, were saved and installed elsewhere under his supervision. All this was followed by widespread speculative purchase. Much Wenlock's Priory buildings and land-holdings were bought in 1545 by the king's Italian physician, Agostino Agostini, (who lived at St Owen's Well House) but he sold them in the same year to a leading local man, Thomas Lawley. Lawley and his descendants lived in the Prior's Lodging which came to be called The Abbey and was regarded as the manor house of Much Wenlock. Intriguingly, the name Lawley still predominates today among Methodist families in the town.

Greater prosperity began to reach Much Wenlock at this time, resulting in part from the increased stability of the Welsh counties under Tudor rule. New charitable institutions were gradually formed to fill at least part of the gap left by the religious orders. However, it is a revealing statistic that, during the reign of Queen Elizabeth (1533-1603) only half the babies born in Much Wenlock lived beyond their childhood.

For almost a thousand years Christianity, led by the Pope in Rome, had dominated the hearts and minds of Europe. But by the beginning of the fifteenth century reform was widely called for and ideas floated as early as John Wyclif, (c.1329-84) the Oxford theologian who had translated the Bible into English and questioned the authority of the Pope, began to circulate more widely. At the beginning of the sixteenth century influential protesant reformers appeared in Switzerland, Bohemia and Saxony and their ideas gained ground across Europe. In England, the Pope's refusal to grant the King a divorce suddenly made rejection of the Pope a political necessity. While the English church continued to support much of Catholic doctrine, the separation from Rome naturally opened the floodgates to more radical protestant thinking. By the seventeenth century puritan ministers were widely active in the Midlands.

(Overleaf) This handsome brass, of 1592, commemorates local squire Richard Ridley, twice Bailiff, and his wife Eleanor, in Holy Trinity Parish Church. The Ridleys were typical of many local families which, all across the country at this period, were able to achieve influential status without the help of noble birth. (Much Wenlock Parish Council)

Neer vnto this place lyeth buried the body of Richard Ridley, S[...]
And heyre of Raynold Rydley of Ipsley Gent, & of Alice leighton hi[...]
wyfe, fyrste Maryed to Thomas Mownslive of Langbley, by whome s[...]
Issue one sonne & v. Daughters, The sayd Richard lived in good nam[...]
Report, & was twyse Bayly of this Towne of Wenlock & y fran[...]
thereof. he maryed Eleanor Daughter of Iohn Sydenham of Childwort[...]
To: Somerset & had no Issue, he Departed out of this transitory lyfe[...]
of Ianuary, 1592, & the sayd Eleanor his wyfe survivyng him, caused[...]
monument to be set vp, for a perpetuall token of her Singuler & obed[...]
wor toward[...]

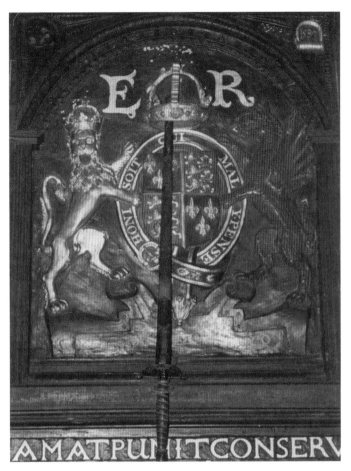

In 1589, after the defeat of the Spanish Armada, one of the high points of the reign of Elizabeth I, her coat-of-arms was installed in the Guildhall. Opposite the lion of England, the red dragon of Wales refers to the Tudor queen's Welsh ancestry. (Much Wenlock Town Council)

In 1672, following the royal Declaration of Indulgence which allowed for a measure of religious tolerance, two Much Wenlock houses were licensed for meetings of Independents. In 1682 eight non-conformists are recorded as living in the town and Henry Maurice, formerly rector of Church Stretton, was licensed as a preacher. During the eighteenth century several meeting-houses are recorded.

The stylish brickwork of the Victorian Methodist chapel.

The influence of Wesleyan preaching was strong in Much Wenlock by the early nineteenth century. In 1862 the Primitive Methodist chapel was established.

Some families, particularly among the gentry, remained loyal to Rome in spite of the disadvantages this brought in that Roman Catholics were debarred from public life. The Lacon family of Linley continued to practise as Catholics and supported small Catholic communities in Linley and Madeley. At Benthall Hall the family were prepared to provide travelling priests with a "priest's hole" where they could hide in case of persecution.

In the later eighteenth century, Roman Catholic baptisms are recorded as having taken place in Much Wenlock and between 1849 and 1852 mass was regularly celebrated here by a priest from Aldenham, near Morville. Local Roman Catholics had to wait until 1955 for the church of St Mary Magdalen to be built at the edge of the town.

Market Town and Borough

After church on Sundays from the earliest times, the space close to Holy Trinity along Barrow Street would have been crowded with people. Many would have travelled in to church from outlying settlements and farms. Inevitably, traders set up stalls and sold their livestock here. The Abbey itself clearly had need of goods and services and naturally became the focus of trade. Small weekly markets at Much Wenlock, dealing in foodstuffs and other goods necessary for daily life, seem to pre-date the Norman Conquest. Hence the open spaces by the church became the core of the trading area, with permanent shops built along the lines of approach. The Bull Ring was a space set aside for the sale or slaughter of bulls and there is no evidence that bull-baiting took place here.

In 1138 King Stephen granted the Priory a three-day fair in June. This was an event with larger appeal, trading in cattle and horses, although no more than twenty animals seem to have been available at any one time. The weekly market was formalised by a grant from Henry III in 1224.

During the fourteenth century it would have been no surprise to encounter in Wenlock's streets well-dressed local businessmen just back from business trips across the Channel. Whilst still paying rents and supplying services to the Priory, by the middle of the thirteenth century the town had managed to establish something of a separate identity. Trade was conducted vigorously, both nationally and on the continent, the destination for much British wool. By now the town was considered quite wealthy.

In 1337 four local merchants, along with men from six other towns, were asked to arrange a loan to the king. It was actually a Wenlock man, Adam atte Home, a merchant trading in wool with Holland,

who supplied the cash. At a time before banks, this suggests no shortage of secure accommodation for gold coinage and the men to protect it.

(Opposite) A busy shop occupies the upper part of the Bull Ring today.

Security was not of course provided by the state and most males would have had a basic idea of physical combat, if only with weapons such as staves and hunting knives. In 1346, along with other Shropshire towns, Wenlock was able to supply four armed men to sail from Portsmouth for the great victory over the French at Crecy.

Children maintaining the ancient pagan tradition of maypole dancing on Church Green (John Morris Jones)

Court Rolls and Charters

At the Norman Conquest, all land was deemed to belong to the sovereign who rewarded his henchmen by allocating to them larger or smaller areas according to the importance of what they could do for him. This was the essence of the feudal system. Land was granted to religious institutions in the same way. Until the Dissolution of the

Monasteries the landowner in the Wenlock area was the Priory and the Prior, as lord of the manor, the principal burgess. Control of crime and the operation of every kind of justice depended on the Prior, who conducted his own court. As the court was the main instrument of local government, the Prior was responsible for all the affairs of the parish, which soon became identified, in terms of its boundaries, with the Borough. The Priory, with holdings of about 9,000 acres, owned a large number of manors, each one of which would be controlled by a Bailiff, responsible to the Prior. (Under the bailiffs were reeves, and from 'shire-reeve' evolved the more familiar word 'sheriff'.)

The Bailiff was the most senior official responsible to the lord of the manor, and conduct of the court, which was the responsibility of the lord, was sometimes delegated to him. While by the time of the later Tudor monarchs, the lord was no longer the Prior, this arrangement continued into the nineteenth century.

The court rolls are the records of the courts and these survive for six of the years between 1344 and 1450. They give a lively picture of economic activity as well as theft, hooliganism and unlawful trading. Interestingly, at least six young local men, who were involved in a violent brawl in 1449, evidently achieved respectability and became civic leaders as they were later to feature prominently in the campaign to achieve the status of borough.

The quarter sessions court (meeting every three months only) dealt with major crimes and could pass sentence of death, which was carried out away from the town "on the Edge Top". By the 1830s, however, such crimes were dealt with elsewhere. The petty sessions courts, which dealt with matters such as licensing, were held at the Raven Inn, which belonged to the landowner George Forester.

The records give frequent insights into the flavour of Wenlock life. In 1805, people were fined by the then presiding authority, who was the major landowner, Sir Watkyn Williams Wynn, for such public offences as having a pig stye in Mardol, setting up a saw-pit and maintaining a stable and dunghill in Wilmore Street. Even at the beginning of the nineteenth century, the town was evidently a noisy, smelly hive of filthy, semi-industrial processes!

The last Bailiff of the town was William Anstice, who became the first Mayor in 1835. Fifty years later the Borough finally lost its MP, fittingly yet another member of the Forester family.

Charters were the means by which communities gradually gained independence from their landlords and study of them is a vital tool of local history. The king would receive cash in return for granting a charter and this is one reason why, in the late twelfth century when he was raising money for the crusades, Richard I gave charters to so many towns, Much Wenlock among them. Wenlock's earliest charters have recently been discovered by the Shropshire historians, Paul Stamper and David Cox. Granted to the Prior in 1138/9, they refer, among other matters, to the court established to provide justice for the Prior's tenants and to the extension of cultivation to hitherto virgin land.

> **(Overleaf) By this Charter, of 1468, Edward IV granted Much Wenlock the status of a free borough. This privilege was secured by a committee of local men led by John Lawley, his son and his grandson, through the agency of Sir John, later Lord, Wenlock, a close friend of Edward IV. Wenlock, whose connections with the town were in fact minimal, was an astute diplomat and public servant. Of dubious integrity, he changed sides during the Wars of the Roses. It is probable that the town of Wenlock supplied men and materials to the Yorkist king during the last months of his war against the Lancastrian party. (Much Wenlock Council)**

The Charter gave the town, in the form of an organised Corporation, freedom from interference by the Sheriff, the most senior county official responsible to the king. It granted to the town the right to hold markets every Monday and a fair in June, as well as control over the price of the basic foodstuffs of bread and ale. These rights,

Edwardus ... in gracia ... presidem ... fidelis Consilium nostri Johes Benlos ... ... stam post sui presenta... ... ... Johm Conestin...

sigillum ... ...
alias villas ... ... Johes ... ...
... ... villis ... ...

with others, amounted to the privilege of raising their own taxes. In addition, the town became responsible for maintaining law and order and was allowed its own gaol for the purpose. Two officials, a bailiff and a coroner, were elected annually. By 1491 the town had two MPs.

Burgesses and Corporation

By 1247 Wenlock had developed its own urban elite in the form of a group of businessmen (burgesses - tenants in a borough), who each paid the rent of one shilling a year to the Priory for "burgage plots" where they both lived and carried on their businesses. These businesses were varied and covered everything required for daily life, from clothing, shoemaking and tool-production to legal and secretarial services. Paper was made at water-powered mills outside the town by the middle of the seventeenth century. At the same time, nail-making is believed to have come here from the West Midlands. In 1808, the town supported two nail shops.

Various building trades were particularly well-represented in Wenlock from the end of the fourteenth century when we hear of William the Carpenter. Later, Richard Dawley (builder of the Guildhall) and his family were well-known carpenters.

Like other medieval towns, the centre of Wenlock was laid out in long, narrow plots fronting the main streets so that occupants could maintain shop fronts while workshop, storage and other activities occupied the rears. These plots were also used for cultivation of food and small livestock, a practice which continued right up until the 1960s. Shop fronts would have had timber shutters which could be let down during opening hours to form trestle-style stalls. For many centuries, a shopping expedition would have been a muddy experience on a wet day it would have involved negotiating discarded offal, vegetable remains and animal dung as well as enduring assorted stenches from the tanneries and brew-houses.

It was from descendants of these trading families that the Corporation was formed when the town was granted Borough status in 1468. This was a particularly significant change as it marked the transfer of power from religious to secular authority. Now the town, as well as controlling markets and the June fair, could elect a Member of Parliament. New responsibilities involved the maintenance of law and order and these brought economic gains in the form of fines and confiscated property, all of which went straight into Borough coffers.

A detail of an early map showing the long and narrow burgage plots.

The power of the church, however, remained a force to be reckoned with and it is illuminating that, in the list of burgesses recorded in the Borough's first Minute book, the name of the Prior, Roger Wenlock, takes first place.

Much Wenlock has always been a small town with (compared to the larger regional centres of Shrewsbury and Ludlow) a relatively limited range of services. However, as early as 1247 it was referred to as a borough, a term which at that period indicated considerable status. During this year, the freemen and burgesses of Wenlock were, in their turn, sufficiently confident and well-organised to complain against their manorial lord, the Prior, and succeed in having an enquiry set up to look into their allegations.

We now expect certain public services to be provided by the local authority but for many centuries the Christian church was the only source of assistance to those who were poor, disabled or sick. In the absence of anything like modern medical knowledge and techniques, life was harsh and often short. Things that we take for granted, such as a supply of clean water, were not always available. The brook flowing down through the town was an open sewer (the Schittebrok) and the earliest public water supply, recorded as such in 1403, was St Milburga's Well.

However, none of this detracted from the perceived dignity of the Borough, demonstrated by its insignia. These were symbols of authority carried and displayed on all official occasions. We do not have the early examples but the existing Serjeant's Mace dates to the seventeenth century, while the other, hallmarked 1811-12, was a gift of George Forester. In addition there are a mid-seventeenth century sword and a set of six staves.

By 1491 Wenlock was entitled to elect two Members of Parliament. As elsewhere, the MPs were mostly drawn from elite local families, in particular the Lawleys of Wenlock Abbey and Spoonhill and the Lacons of Willey. The latter are an intriguing example of the way Roman Catholics, who were officially debarred from public office of any kind, sometimes managed to retain a very mainstream role in public life. In 1592, however, the rise of the new middle class was making itself felt in Much Wenlock in the person of the new Bailiff, Christopher Morrall, a tanner.

By 1618 the Weld family was established at the nearby estate of Willey and they and the Foresters, united later through marriage into one family, were to dominate the political scene for two hundred and fifty years. Because of the economic dependency of large numbers of rural tenants on the great estates feudal practices and attitudes survived well into the nineteenth century, some even into the twentieth. For this reason the Forester family, which had made money from the development of the coalfield, was easily able to persuade the electorate to return its candidates to Parliament. Weld-Foresters therefore provided the Borough with Conservative MPs for most of Queen Victoria's reign.

The Corporation also had a seal, dating to the latter part of the fifteenth century, showing the Holy Trinity, St Milburga with a bishop's crozier and book, and St Michael. Lord Wenlock's escutcheon appears below, alongside the rampant lion of his patron, Edward IV and the white hart of Roger of Montgomery. (Much Wenlock Council)

The Borough functioned effectively, administering its large and somewhat dispersed territory for several centuries. This was interrupted only by incidents such as the absconding, in 1606, of the Treasurer, the weaver Richard Crippyn, who had helped himself to £40 of the town's funds, a huge sum for the time.

Apart from the instances referred to earlier of armed men being sent to assist the king on some occasions, military matters were never high on the agenda of this rural district. Nevertheless, it did share in the wave of panic that swept the nation at the end of the eighteenth

The timber-framed Guildhall, "buildid over ye Prisonne" is supported on massive oak struts. Upstairs can be seen the ancient Court of Assize chamber with its Bench. Above hangs the symbolic Sword of Justice and the Royal Arms of 1589. Walking through to the next room visitors can see the Council Chamber, which is still used by the present Council. (Gordon Dickins)

century when invasion by the French armies of Napoleon was widely feared. The Loyal Wenlock Infantry, like other more-or-less private militias, was established by local gentry from among their employees and tenants, but it existed only between 1799 and 1805.

This episode was echoed in the time of Napoleon III when the Wenlock Rifle Volunteer Corps came into being in 1859; this body was to survive for fifty years.

Wenlock Volunteers' jug, made by John Rose and Co of Coalport. between 1800 and 1806. Bearing the slogan "Success to the Wenlock Volunteers", this jug would have been used on the regimental mess table. (Shropshire Regimental Museum)

Looking at the modest country town that is Much Wenlock today, it is extraordinary to reflect that it was the largest county Borough in the whole of England for several hundred years. However, as an administrative unit it eventually became unsatisfactory because of demographic and other changes. The Borough was finally dissolved in 1966 as part of general local government reorganisation and control passed to the present local authority, Bridgnorth District Council.

Wenlock's Setting: Farming and Rural Life

In Saxon times vast tracts of land were uncultivated forest or scrub and, as the population grew, these areas were gradually brought under the plough. Much Wenlock would have formed a small nucleus of farming activity amid woodland, used for grazing, with the land becoming over distance ever wilder and denser.

Before woodland clearance began to take place on any extensive scale, large wooded areas acted as boundaries between parishes and manors. The boundary between Callaughton and Acton Round in Spoonhill Wood, for example, was fixed and generally accepted by 1256.

The woods themselves were considered to be freely available to local smallholders as grazing areas, in particular for pigs, which were a valuable source of meat through the winter. In 1086 Much Wenlock manor had woodland (in particular Westwood along the Edge) for the grazing of up to three hundred pigs, but by the thirteenth century some clearing of woodland to create more agricultural land had taken place. Some cleared woods became common grazing land, or land used by groups of people. Individuals, however, as records show, did frequently clear woodland for private agricultural purposes.

Woods were, of course, the main source of fuel for heating and cooking universally, and lack of access to such fuel meant the direst poverty and suffering. In 1557 the woodward, an official employed by the Borough to care for and maintain the woodland, is recorded as authorising the felling and sale of a hundred old trees to the poor for fuel.

Until 1301, the Shirlett area was a royal forest for hunting, extending 20km from Buildwas on the Severn to Aston Botterell in the south.

The much reduced core of this old forest is now managed carefully and its ancient trees preserved. In Tudor times it was a "waste", largely available as common land for cottagers to graze pigs.

Remains of the great medieval forest of Shirlett can be seen on high ground beyond this gate.

In the early medieval period the land which formed the Priory's manor, around Much Wenlock, was divided into four large fields, Spittle, Edge (or west), South, and Pertley. These were farmed on the strip system of rotated crops. Individual tenants would have crofts, or smallholdings, next to their homes which they could farm as they wished, but the open fields, where they might hold twenty acres each, were farmed communally. Apart from wheat, the crops were spring-sown mixed grains, oats and barley, peas, vetches and beans. Hay would be made annually for winter fodder for sheep, horses and cattle.

Revolt

Although we know little of the lives of peasant farmers, an extraordinary and unique event took place in Much Wenlock in 1163, mirroring in microcosm the Peasants' Revolt of nearly two hundred years later. The villeins, a term referring to the lowest social status above that of serf, formed the majority of the population. They were rent-paying tenants who could own land and oxen (the only source of motive power, apart from donkeys and the far more costly horse, in medieval Europe) but were required to work for their lord. Without warning, it seems, the villeins of Wenlock rose up, appealing to the king for the removal of the Prior. They "threw down their ploughshares", and when, in church, they were declared excommunicated, a frightening state of affairs at that time, they besieged the church and fought back with vigour against some knights who tried to restore order. The Prior was forced to hold an enquiry and to accept the decisions taken by the committee, made up of four knights and six monks, which had been agreed to by the villeins. This incident illustrates the growing economic power of this class who were able to expand their landholdings and, eventually, employ labour themselves and demand cash for their services to the Prior.

Common Land Enclosure

Although parts of Much Wenlock parish still had open fields in 1722 the process of enclosure, whereby individuals took possession of land hitherto farmed communally, had been gaining ground since 1517 when a commission reported on enclosure in Shropshire. The last open field land was enclosed as a consequence of Act of Parliament in 1775, although two large commons remained available for livestock grazing and fuel collecting. One result was that local people who had hitherto had the right to graze livestock in the Shirlett woods were no longer allowed to do so. Increasingly, small farms were bought by larger ones.

This was also a period when landowners such as the Foresters were re-organising their holdings, often by means of exchange, to create more viable estates and facilitate more efficient farming methods.

Livestock and Hunting

During the period when the land belonged largely to the monastery, it was farmed by lay brothers and partly let out to small tenants who probably also worked in various capacities as servants to the monks. Together with the pigs mentioned earlier, there would have been high concentrations of livestock, including oxen for heavy work.

In 1291 the Prior had a herd of twenty-five cows and a flock of nearly a thousand wool-producing sheep, of which a quarter were breeding ewes. He also had a stable of nineteen mares for breeding. For the production of high quality foals he may have used a travelling stallion from one of the FitzAlan studs, such as the one named Morel Lestrange (FitzAlan family names), which we know fulfilled this function in the thirteenth century.

Horses were important transport and pack animals with a higher status than oxen and many varieties were required, from the heaviest draught horse to the light lady's palfrey and the fast hunter. Hunting was, from the dawn of human history, a vital part of maintaining a good diet and it retained this function for the poor (who were forced to do it illegally, as poaching). For the wealthy it became a pastime related to war, in which men, their horses and their dogs, could demonstrate courage, stamina and skill in pursuit of deer and the ferocious boar. The word 'forest' itself signified an area set aside for hunting.

Within the forest of Shirlett lay the Prior's own wood, covering most of the south-western part. Hunting was dear to the hearts of many high-ranking clergy and woodland was maintained for this purpose on their estates. In 1252 Prior Humbert paid three hundred marks for royal assent to enclose a deer park at the manor of Oxenbold, and he entertained the Bishop of Hereford at his hunting-lodge here in 1290. The Bishop's retinue included thirty-five horses.

Hunting continued to be a major concern of the wealthy, its physical challenges being seen as a good preparation for soldiery. John Weld, an important local example of the rise of the entrepreneurial middle class in the seventeenth century (see p54) became squire of Willey and bought deer to stock the park. George Forester, the Hunting Squire, who died in 1811, maintained a famous pack of foxhounds along with large numbers of horses (including, so local tradition alleges, a horseriding mistress) on Shirlett Common.

The Forester's Lodge at Millichope was built in the twelfth century as base for an official employed by the king to maintain forest law. Built of stone it has a fortress-like air and contains a gaol for poachers and other offenders. (Paul Stamper)

From the middle of the nineteenth century, cattle took over from sheep as the main livestock bred locally, although the Shropshire Down remained an important breed until the early twentieth century. Most cattle were bred for beef as delivering dairy produce on more than a local scale was difficult before motor transport and refrigeration.

Agricultural Change

Farms were of all sizes until, in the eighteenth century, larger farms began to take over the small ones which, earlier, might have been the property of town tradesmen. This was a period when ambitious men, who had made money in London, began to buy landed estates. Existing landowners, extended their estates by judicious purchase, especially if their prosperity had been boosted by valuable mineral deposits, as had the Foresters' here.

During the eighteenth century, alongside the new industrial developments, major improvements took place in agriculture. Land and the countryside had always been economically and emotionally important to the English upper class and now gentlemen farmers began to take an interest in the breeding and improvement of livestock. Many of the breeds of British farm animal that we know today, such as Hereford cattle, were developed and defined during this period. In the land surrounding Much Wenlock a number of nationally respected herds were developed, including Jersey and Ayrshire cattle.

Wenlock Avenger, a magnificent stallion from the Milners' shire horse stud at Callaughton, where the same family still farms. One of Shropshire's most important products, historically, was the warhorse, bred extensively in the county by the FitzAlan family. (This family, now headed by the Duke of Norfolk, based at Arundel Castle in Sussex, later relinquished its ties with Shropshire.) Contrary to popular belief the chargers used by knights in battle would not have been as large as shire horses although they would have been sturdy and brave. (Photo by kind permission of Mr and Mrs Milner)

Farming has always been subject to fluctuations in prosperity and, during the Napoleonic wars, the rise in prices and rents led to an increase in cereal production as this was cheaper than livestock farming. By 1813, 60% of the farmland of the manor of Wenlock was arable. Wheat and barley were grown as cash crops, although by the late nineteenth century oats had become more important, sown in rotation with root vegetables and clover for animal feed. During the 1870s, when over half of Shropshire was owned by large estates of at least 3,000 acres, agriculture was hit by a major depression which, combined with outbreaks of animal diseases, took its toll among the poorest workers. The availability of farm work continued to decline until the beginning of the nineteenth century. Those who did have work were often in severe poverty, living in tied cottages which lacked even the most basic facilities, even though some landowners did try to improve the conditions of their workforce. In response to low wages, a farmers' union was established for south Shropshire in 1871, but because of the wide dispersal of the membership and difficulties of communication, little was achieved.

It is interesting that the novelist Thomas Hardy, who writes of agricultural conditions at this period, visited Much Wenlock, staying at the Prior's Lodging as guest of the Milnes Gaskells. A writer much concerned with the decline of the old rural traditions and certainties, he would have been aware of particular cases of hardship in the Shropshire countryside.

During and after the last War, farming was heavily subsidised but over-production resulted and the situation is now very different. By 1965 barley had taken over as the main cereal crop, and most of the grain was marketed in Liverpool and Manchester, providing work for local haulage firms. Haulage and fuel costs have since risen, threatening this form of employment. Increasingly, too, as farmers are required to keep more and more detailed records, small farms cannot survive. At the close of the twentieth century, following public anxiety over outbreaks of so-called Mad Cow Disease and other food scares, farming entered a severe depression, which at the time of writing has been exacerbated by an outbreak of Foot-and Mouth

Disease. The role of the countryside in the twenty-first century remains uncertain and problematic.

More and more town-dwellers are choosing to move to the countryside and immense new housing schemes will expand small towns such as Much Wenlock. The results of these demographic changes on the rural landscape remain to be seen.

(Opposite) A farmer and his stockman (wearing the traditional countryman's smock) admire their Herefords at Buildwas Abbey (Shrewsbury Museums)

(Overleaf) Log cutting at the beginning of the last century in Much Wenlock. These men are employees of the Milnes Gaskell family who became owners of the Abbey and manor in 1857. The timber, felled in the autumn in estate woodland, would have been brought to the town by teams of heavy horses. Here a portable steam engine, similar to others now used throughout farming, provides power for the saw. (SCC)

Much Wenlock during the Civil War

For modern visitors travelling along the Wenlock Edge road, it is easy to spot an opening in the woodland and a large flat limestone rock. It is worth stopping here to see the glorious view of the Ape Dale spread below, quite apart from the incident that tradition tells us took place here. Now known as Major's Leap, this was the site of an amazing escape during the English Civil War. A young Royalist, Major Thomas Smallman of Wilderhope Manor, pursued by Parliamentarian soldiers in a furious chase, leapt off this rock on the back of what must have been either a staggeringly courageous or a rather dim horse. The charger was, of course, killed, but the Major was thrown into a thornbush and escaped his pursuers at the cost of a few scratches!

Wilderhope Manor built in 1586, is one of a series of large farm houses in the Much Wenlock area demonstrating the prosperity of sheep producers in the heyday of the wool trade. The dark limestone of its construction is majestically enhanced by its lonely Corve Dale location. Now a Youth Hostel, it was the model for Undern Hall in the film of Mary Webb's novel Gone to Earth. (Roy Penhallurick)

The English Civil War was a conflict involving a number of complex issues, some not resolved for more than a hundred years. It began with a dispute between Charles I (who reigned from 1625-1645) and his Parliament, which in England had developed considerable authority. On one hand, therefore, stood a monarch whose managerial talents were weak but who combined financial extravagance with an unshakeable belief in his own Divine Right to rule. On the other side stood a confident and articulate Parliament, which the king had attempted to bypass and which suspected him of harbouring deeply unpopular Roman Catholic leanings.

The protestantism which had swept Europe at the time of the Reformation had become firmly established in these islands, especially among the upwardly-mobile merchant class, but this class, nevertheless, remained politically conservative and was far from unanimous in supporting the final execution of the king.

The Midlands played a large part in the Civil War and, although Shropshire's role was apparently a minor one, control of the county's resources, communications and main towns, was critical. Shrewsbury and Bridgnorth were important centres for both armies. The town of Much Wenlock, sandwiched between these garrisons, apparently did its best to maintain a low profile, although some involvement was unavoidable.

A successful iron furnace, for example, at Bouldon, not far from Munslow, produced 63 tons of ordnance for the King's cause, delivering it to Bridgnorth and Shrewsbury. In 1644 the furnace's clerk was asked to produce a similar quantity, including a cannon, for the defence of Ludlow.

The parish registers for Much Wenlock, described in a royal charter of 1631 as a "great, old and populous village", give only the names of three or four soldiers. However, as a contemporary document from the north Shropshire village of Myddle shows, families in such small places were often torn apart by the wars which took many ordinary people's lives and livelihoods. A newspaper report of 29 October, 1642, states that "taxes, billeting of soldiers and plundering of men's houses, hath quite undone the whole county of Shropshire (which) is so impoverished with the robbings and ransackings of these Rebels..."

This engraving of 1779 shows the Abbey in ruins. (SCC)

Of the twelve Shropshire members of the Long Parliament (so-called because it sat from 1639 to 1660) eight supported the king. Other members of the local gentry did so too. Chatwell Hall, near Cardington, which had been enlarged by Thomas Corfield in 1613, was fortified by his son Richard and defended against Parliamentarian attack in the Civil War. Nevertheless, puritan and Parliamentarian sympathisers were to be found throughout the mercantile classes and some of the most able belonged to the gentry. In April 1642 Parliament appointed a committee "for the association of the counties of Warwick, Stafford and Salop (Shropshire)" consisting of the leading local opponents of the king.

The king came to Shrewsbury from Oxford and stayed there for three months, during which time his better-off supporters brought in their silver plate to be melted down for coinage with which to pay the army. This period, during which the troops were billeted, uninvited, on local civilians, must have strained royalist sympathies severely.

Charles left Shrewsbury on 12 October 1642 and stayed the night in Much Wenlock, sleeping, according to legend, at the Blue Bridge Inn, now Ashfield Hall. At that time, the population is estimated as being between six and seven hundred.

In 1645 a cavalry skirmish brought victory to Sir William Vaughan, the Royalist commander, and later on in the same year the rearguard of the king's troops spent the night here, again en route for Bridgnorth. It was in the same year, though, that the Royalist cause began to fail and, within weeks of the fall of Shrewsbury Castle, Benthall Hall had been taken for Parliament. This event will have had great impact locally and convinced people that the king's cause was lost. Soon Ludlow, the last important Royalist stronghold, was to collapse, taken by the Parliamentarian general Sir William Brereton at the end of May.

It is difficult to establish what life must have been like for ordinary townsfolk at this disturbed period. For many, the routines of farming or business may have been maintained smoothly enough. At least by the end of the war conditions cannot have been all gloom and evidently allowed certain entertainers to make a living; in 1649 we find a fiddler, Abraham Lloyd, settled in the parish.

Wenlock largely escaped the ravages of the Civil War. Benthall Hall, however, where visitors may still see the secret hiding place provided by the family for a Roman Catholic priest, saw some fighting when it was taken by a small Parliamentarian force. Benthall is one of a series of handsome, stone-built Elizabethan manors constructed in the hinterland of Wenlock during the period of Tudor prosperity. Others are Shipton Hall and Wilderhope. (Roy Penhallurick)

Commerce, Trade and Industry

Industrial Development

Shropshire was to become the scene of the most significant industrial change during the mid-eighteenth century and for thirty years or so after that was the country's major iron-producing area. Its geological riches, however, had led to the development of industry here centuries earlier.

Walkers on the Edge can often come across the remains of quarries and kilns, which illustrate how busy the area once was. In the medieval period, limestone was quarried at a series of sites on this side of the town. Building lime was a resource well enough sought after for, in 1399, large quantities had to be transported as far as twenty miles across the county, to Caus Castle, near the Welsh border. During the Tudor period the same material helped in the building of Shrewsbury School. Lime-burning, the process by which powdery lime was produced from solid rock, was an activity easy enough to engage in without being properly authorised in the privacy of the forests, and the authorities were forever trying to bring it under control.

The earliest record of coalmining, which was to become so important for Shropshire, appears in 1322 when Walter of Caldebrok rented a shed to dig for coal, at le Brockhole, (from its name, evidently a former badger sett). In 1394 Richard II authorised a certain James Mynour, of Derby, to mine for copper and silver on Priory land. Nothing seems to have come of this venture. In the century after 1570, however, the uses of coal began to increase. It was used across east Shropshire for smelting lead ore, salt- and tar-making, firing clay tobacco pipes and domestic pottery, and glassmaking. Early in the eighteenth century there was a huge expansion of coalmining in the parishes of Broseley, Madeley and Benthall. In 1708-9 the first great innovation of the Industrial Revolution took place with Abraham

Darby's pioneering use of coke produced from coal, used instead of charcoal for the smelting of iron.

Shropshire was also important as a source of iron, and the first blast furnace, using charcoal and limestone with water-powered bellows, was operating on Shirlett Common during the 1540s. The extremely uneven terrain in the woods there is a legacy of exhaustive lime-digging and burning which went on along with coppicing, a form of woodland management where trees are cut to just above the base and allowed to re-sprout on multiple stems. These stems, or 'poles', were cut and used for several purposes including charcoal and pit-props in the mines. Charcoal was produced from wood of at least twenty years' growth and therefore plenty of trees were required. However, as industrial methods became more efficient and charcoal used less, the land on which these trees were grown came to be more highly valued for growing other crops.

During the twentieth century, limestone quarrying, largely for road-building, continued to be a major source of employment, stimulated in the second half of the century by the creation of Telford New Town. However, this particular demand has all but ceased. Any observant driver along the Stretton Road can see how heavily the Edge has been quarried and in recent years environmental concerns have limited the quarries' output. Stone haulage, however, remains a major part of local heavy traffic.

John Weld d.1666

Many ambitious men who had made money through business began to acquire estates in the seventeenth century. In 1618 John Weld, a rich lawyer from Cheshire, who had managed to buy the office of Town Clerk of London, began to purchase large swathes of the Shropshire coalfield, including the manors of Marsh and Broseley and the estate of Willey. Anxious to run the estate in the traditional way, he bought deer, swans, fish and bees and established horse-breeding. Knighted in 1642, he was clever enough to avoid any problems during the Civil War and died after the Restoration of Charles II, in 1666. Weld was extremely able and intelligent, foreseeing features of the Industrial Revolution such as the smelting of iron with coal, and he left to his descendants one of the largest landholdings of the area.

Weld's granddaughter and heir, Elizabeth, married Brooke Forester, whose business partner was the ironmaster John Wilkinson. Together, these two men formed the New Willey Company in 1757 and leased part of the old park at Willey to create a furnace, powered by the fishponds, for ironworkings. A horse-drawn waggon, running on iron rails, was an innovation which took their products to the river Severn at Jackfield. From here they could be transported on barges to Bristol and thence exported almost anywhere.

As a result of the huge expansion of the Industrial Revolution, a number of smaller hamlets around Much Wenlock, now no longer recognisable as such, emerged in response to the demand for limestone and its transport to the river. One such, referred to then as the New Town, on the Stretton Road, is now thoroughly integrated into Wenlock itself. Slightly further off, Farley, on the Buildwas road, developed at the beginning of the nineteenth century. By 1841 most of its householders were waggoners, hauling stone to the river. These businesses provided work for two wheelwrights and no less than four blacksmiths. Perhaps not surprisingly, there were two alehouses here.

Trade and Businesses

In spite of the prosperity of the quarries, however, from the second half of the sixteenth century and into the seventeenth, the main industry and trade of Much Wenlock involved woollen cloth. There were cloth-workers of all kinds here; haberdashers, who dealt in smaller clothing items, drapers, who were wholesalers, mercers (general merchants), as well as the odd cap and hat-maker. By 1841 there were as many as fourteen tailors working in the town.

Leather was another local industry; tanning depended partly on the presence of lime and bark, both plentifully available locally. From the sixteenth century until Victorian times there are records of several tanning businesses in Much Wenlock. Tanning was practised in 1221, and subsidiary trades were carried on too. A glover, a weaver and a shearer were living here in 1327. All these men would have had workshops employing others and of course offering training. In the second half of the sixteenth century Wenlock had at least four glovers. It was sometimes possible for women to maintain businesses of their own, and a tannery, on the north side of what is now the upper High Street, was operated until 1710 by a widow, Anne Hancocks.

Felted woollen caps like the one shown here were universally worn. We know that in 1661 there was a feltmaker living and working in Much Wenlock. (Rowley's House Museum)

In 1841 there were no fewer than twenty-five shoemakers working in Wenlock, and ten years later three saddlers are recorded. Their work would have covered making and repair of draught horse harness as well as other leather products. Blacksmithing was a necessary and popular trade and there were several forges in the town.

Building was a trade well represented in Wenlock in Tudor times when prosperity allowed many families to construct or re-build impressive homes. Clearly the technical expertise to enable this to happen was available and we know, for example, that nails were made locally for many generations. The first carpenter to appear in the records is one William, mentioned in 1386, and in the early years of the sixteenth century Walter Wilcock was employed as a carpenter by the Priory. By this time surnames had come into more general use and his colleague, Clement Mason, like many others, was known by the name of his trade. The very able mason, Walter Hancox, who died in 1599, achieved a reputation as an architect and is thought to have designed and constructed Condover Hall and the Shrewsbury Market Hall.

Later, brickmaking became a local trade and brick kilns were widespread, remembered in some local place names, such as Brick Yard and Brick Leasow.

The Wenlock windmill, wrecked by lightning in 1850, is a much-loved local landmark. A trust has now been formed to preserve it. (Suzanne Boulos)

Tobacco smoking was widely enjoyed by both sexes and, while Broseley was the main local pipe-making centre (with, now, an attractive museum devoted to the industry) Wenlock had two pipe-makers by 1650. Twenty-five years later pipes were considered to be the town's chief manufacture. An observant walker in fields around the town today can usually pick up, along with a variety of pottery shards, pieces of clay pipe.

For centuries, small market towns had to supply every personal and household need. Between 1642-59, we even find evidence of a clockmaker in Much Wenlock, Richard Byrd; and in 1578 Thomas Simons ran a pewterer's business here. Farley had its own frying-pan shop in 1790.

Mills operated by water for a variety of tasks, including paper-making at Farley, were a common sight from early medieval times and the remaining windmill, its stonework now thought to date from the seventeenth century, probably milled malt.

Another lively business was brewing. Because of the impurity of much of the water, a mild ale was drunk by everyone right up to the Victorian era (by which time tea had become the universal beverage). In 1614 Much Wenlock had twenty-one alesellers, all of whom would have brewed their own stock. Brewing was a trade in which women were well represented at this time. Before mechanisation, brewing could be carried out on a small scale and it provided an income for widows and other women on their own. There were at least four malthouses in 1714, where hops for ale-making were laid out to dry. A hundred years later the number had gone up to eleven. One of these was the building to the rear of The Talbot pub.

In 1769 Thomas Littlehales was producing around 2000 bushels of malt a season in the Bull Ring. Mechanised commercial brewing did not begin until 1894, when the former Sheinton Street Tannery was converted to the Wheatland Brewery, which survived into the 1920s. Before the coming of the railway made communication easier (and indeed, after this) the role of the public house was crucial in market towns. Much business was transacted in inns, particularly those that offered overnight accommodation for travelling businessmen and their horses.

In Much Wenlock, the leading hostelries during the heyday of coaching at the beginning of the nineteenth century were the Wynnstay Arms (now the Gaskell Arms) and the Fox (now the Wheatland Fox) which were close to the important coach route to Shrewsbury. Other public houses were the Talbot and its near neighbour the White Hart (now gone), and the Fox and the Raven (now the Raven) in Barrow Street. These hostelries provided a range of functions for the community; in 1697 the county quarter sessions met by adjournment at the Talbot.

A modern historical pageant taking place outside the malthouse at the Talbot, now bed and breakfast accommodation. (Suzanne Boulos)

A decorative plaque records the building of a house in the High Street.

Beer was brewed at the George and Dragon pub as recently as the 1950s. The popular perry, or pear cider, a seemingly innocuous brew — until you got up to walk — was known as "tanglelegs"!

Victorian Wenlock

The population of Much Wenlock, nearly two thousand at the beginning of the nineteenth century, had increased by 28% seventy years later. This followed a general pattern as towns became more and more centres of all kinds of activity and employment, from blacksmithing to libraries.

Certain trades which had been active in the town declined in the nineteenth century. These included clock, watch and needle making, and the manufacture of the ubiquitous clay pipe. What came to replace them were professions and services. Apothecaries (chemists) and surgeons (who did not always enjoy the respect later accorded to the medical profession) had existed here since the eighteenth century. By 1798 legal services were provided by a partnership of two attorneys. But, as the accession of Queen Victoria approached, there were new services such as a printing press, set up in Wilmore Street by Thomas Lawley in 1835. Financial services became more widely available with a bank in Barrow Street and the Wenlock Franchise Savings Bank. This building, now an elegant private house, can still be seen, standing on the left as you walk down the Bull Ring. Together with its Ironbridge branch, this bank had nearly two thousand investors in 1850, reflecting both prosperity and the new bourgeois values of prudence and thrift.

While the town enjoyed these amenities, life in rural England at this time was often far from idyllic. Many villages in Victorian England were under the total control of powerful landowners or local squires. These were known as 'closed' villages, while 'open' villages were owned by small individual freeholders. Much Wenlock, in the latter group, offered living accommodation for very poor or migrant labourers, some from Ireland, who would walk to work on outlying farms.

The great estates were largely worked by their own staffs, living in tied cottages, but on these, and the smaller farms, there was always a need for extra seasonal labour. The simple limestone cottages around Much Wenlock, extending to the so-called New Town along the Stretton road, were densely occupied in this way; living conditions were insanitary and squalid. A government enquiry in 1869, when concerns about public health were widespread, reported that labourers' cottages in Shropshire were poorer than in any other county except Dorset.

The Squatter's Cottage, built between sunrise and sunset by homeless labourers, to take advantage of Squatters' Rights and gain a permanent footing in the town. (Suzanne Boulos)

Rural poverty went hand-in-hand with ignorance and superstition. The fatal stabbing in 1857 of an old woman by her much younger lover perpetuated the stories of witchcraft. Nanny Morgan had been in great demand for her story-telling but, after her murder, all who had known her testified to her possession of the 'evil eye'. The Mayor went so far as to decree that all the witch's belongings should be publicly burnt. Yet this was only a couple of years before the arrival of that symbol of modernity, the railway.

Soon after Queen Victoria acceded to the throne, in 1835, as a result of the Municipal Corporations Act, Much Wenlock acquired its first Mayor, William Anstice. He had been the last man to hold the ancient office of Bailiff, which had been established nearly four hundred years earlier. This legislation, intended to rationalise local government, also deprived Much Wenlock of its detached parts, more than a third of its territory.

Social class and money continued to dictate much of the life of the town. By the beginning of the nineteenth century Much Wenlock was still unable to offer any education to people unable to pay quite large school fees. Such children had to wait until 1847 when a National School was founded, in the building now known as the Priory Hall, close to the parish church. Fees were not abolished altogether until 1891. Early in the twentieth century two small 'dame' or nursery schools existed, one in Mardol Cottage and the other at Milburga's Cottage in Barrow Street.

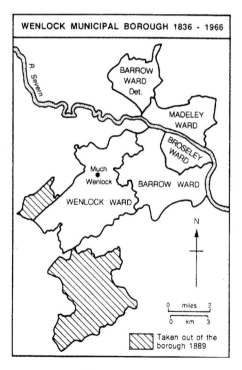

Wenlock Borough 1836-1966 showing the five new wards created for the Borough.

The Shropshire market towns which thrived during the nineteenth century were those served by the railway, which was brought here by the Much Wenlock and Severn Junction Railway Company in 1862. A horse-operated railtrack had served industrial purposes for many years. Now local limestone could be easily transported to West Midlands ironworks or down river to those at Ironbridge. By 1864 passengers could travel from Much Wenlock to Hereford and Birmingham and thence onwards to London.

A Victorian photograph of the Station (now a private house) shows a train arriving.

Lady Catherine Milnes-Gaskell

While for generations Much Wenlock had not been much noticed by what was called polite society, by the middle of the nineteenth century it had a proper gentleman's country seat in the shape of the old Prior's Lodging (called The Abbey), where the owner, C.G. Milnes-Gaskell and his talented and energetic wife, Lady Catherine, received a series of distinguished guests. Among these were the novelist Thomas Hardy (1840-1928) and his wife Emma, the explorer Stanley, and the Arts and Crafts architect Philip Webb, who worked on several commissions in Shropshire. Perhaps their best-known foreign visitor was the American novelist Henry James (1843-1916) who visited in 1877, 1878 and 1882.

He wrote part of 'The Turn of the Screw' here and, in 'The Princess Casamassima', of 1886, he describes a house probably based on the Prior's Lodging. Lady Catherine Milnes-Gaskell writes with charming, if sometimes sentimental, nostalgia about life in and around Wenlock in her two books, 'Spring in a Shropshire Abbey' and 'Old Shropshire Life'. In the first of these, she refers to a family friend, the famous Wenlockian, novelist and poet, Mary Webb (1881-1927).

Lady Catherine was a gifted needlewoman as well as a writer. This tapestry, which she created in the style of the great Victorian designer William Morris, hangs in the Parish Church today. (Much Wenlock Parish Council)

Mary Webb spent her early life at the Grange, on Wenlock Edge, and was profoundly influenced by the beauty of the landscape and the wild natural life which surrounded her. She was fascinated by ancient customs which she could see were fast vanishing and records picturesque characters such as John Lloyd, the Beadle of Much Wenlock church whom she knew as a child of ten, when he was nearly a hundred. She writes nostalgically of her visits to read the Bible to him, always the same choice of passage, in 'Many Mansions'.

"Here was John, in his Windsor chair, his black and yellow wand beside him, his great black Bible so heavy that it made my arms ache, ready on the deal table."

Mary Webb's first collection of poems and essays, 'The Spring of Joy', was published in 1917 and she went on to produce a series of remarkable novels set in the Shropshire countryside before her premature death. 'Gone to Earth', perhaps her most famous novel, was filmed in Much Wenlock.

Commemorative plaque to Mary Webb behind the Guildhall (Suzanne Boulos)

Wenlock Olympians

The Victorian period saw a most extraordinary lift for the fortunes and morale of Much Wenlock in the person of William Penny Brookes (1809-1895). Possessed of huge energy, this local doctor was determined to bring new life to the town's economy, public health and social life. Involved in establishing the railway and a local gasworks, he is remembered locally for the building of the Corn Exchange and the creation of both a library and a museum. His most notable achievement, however, remains the contribution he made to the revival of the Greek Olympic Games and the creation of the modern Olympics.

In 1841 Brookes and his brother founded the Wenlock Agricultural Reading Society, aimed at offering a means of self-education to poor farmers and labourers. From this grew a number of other ventures, of which the Olympian Society was the most popular and enduring.

The Corn Market, (now known as the Corn Exchange) designed by the Shropshire architect S. Pountney Smith in 1852, provided a library, museum and reading room on the first floor. Its main function was as a much-needed covered space for the sale of grain. (John Morris Jones)

Much Wenlock already had its own cricket team in 1841 but Penny Brookes, convinced of the importance of the Greek ideal of all-round physical and mental health, introduced the Olympian Games in 1850. The early sporting events run by the Olympian Society have a distinctly quaint aspect, with blindfold wheelbarrow races, but as time went on

a serious athletic character developed which attracted competitors from far afield. Greek ideals were reflected in the style of the Games; winners received laurel crowns and were regaled with odes composed in their honour. International recognition came in 1890 with the visit of Baron Pierre de Coubertin, founder of the modern Olympics, who publicly acknowledged the inspiration provided by the Wenlock Olympian Society. This was confirmed by his successor, Juan Antonio de Samaranch, when he visited Much Wenlock in 1992.

The Games were held on the seven-acre Linden Field, owned by the Milnes-Gaskell family, who in 1935 presented it to the town. This magnificent space, referred to still as the Games Ground, with its attractive backdrop of trees, has been a huge asset to the town. It is now jointly used by Shropshire County Council and the William Brookes School.

(Opposite) Much Wenlock Olympian Games, Whit Tuesday 1887. Charles Ainsworth of Spoonhill receives the laurel crown of ancient Greek tradition from Miss Marian Serjeantson of Acton Burnell. The Society's founder, Dr William Penny Brookes, wears medals awarded by various athletic societies. The Herald, rather oddly, wears hired 'Tudor' dress.

Dr William Penny Brookes.

Ashfield Hall.

Buildings

Much Wenlock's High Street has considerable charm, dependent on a variety of building periods and styles which, nevertheless, somehow seem to come together in a harmonious mixture. The upper High Street, known as Spittle (or Hospital) Street, appears to have been developed in the Tudor period and a row of cruck cottages of that date are Listed, opposite Ashfield Hall. Cruck construction depends on a pair of curved timbers placed together to form an arch.

This building method can be seen in the gable end of St Owen's Cottage, adjoining St Owen's Well. During the 1540s this was the home of the priest William Corvehill. It was provided for him as part of his salary. (Suzanne Boulos)

Ashfield Hall, mentioned in 1421, was built by William Ashfield, who was living in Much Wenlock in 1396. It may have been the site of the former St John's Hospital for "lost and naked beggars". The timber-framed section was probably built by the locally important Lawley family, who bought the Priory estate after the Dissolution of the Monasteries. Slightly later, in 1554, it was the scene of a magnificent banquet in honour of the Lord President of the Council of the Marches, whose base was at Ludlow Castle. The house has had a chequered history, becoming the Blue Bell Inn and later a lodging-house for itinerant labourers. In about 1853 it was bought by William Penny Brookes.

(Opposite) Raynald's Mansion is the most imposing timber-framed house in Much Wenlock, its frontage dating from 1600. John Raynalds added the three bays and balconies to the front eighty-two years later. Like many other buildings in Wenlock it incorporates a medieval hall.

(photograph by kind permission of Mr John King)

Although Raynald's Mansion is now an antique shop, less genteel aspects of its commercial past are revealed in the various hooks and bars over the doors and the post and rail by the door to help a carrier lift a heavy load onto his back. Later it became a shop for a butcher whose meat was slaughtered only a few hundred yards away in Sheinton Street. The building's elegant frontage was superimposed on the medieval structure in 1682.

The Corn Exchange, paid for by public subscription organised by William Penny Brookes, was erected in 1852 on land given by Sir Watkyn Williams Wynn. This form of public building, with its Italian-style arcaded loggia, introduced a new sophistication to the town. It still offers covered space for various markets, including stalls for charities and the regular weekly market organised by the Women's Institute. Upstairs it housed the library of the Wenlock Agricultural Reading Society.

The present Guildhall building (see p33) dates from 1577. Its original function, in 1540, was to provide a courthouse at the dissolution of the Priory. Below was the medieval stone gaol, and the splendid Council Chamber, still in use, was "buildid over ye prisonne" as part of a scheme of enlargement to accommodate record-keeping and meetings of the Council. The ancient Court of Assize chamber, with the Bench where the judge sat, is open to the public. Overhead hang the Sword of Justice and the royal arms of 1589. Visitors can walk through to the Council Chamber, adorned with decorative panelling and furniture in seventeenth century style installed there by the town's Victorian benefactor, William Penny Brookes. The open space underneath is used regularly for an antique market.

Next to the Abbey ruins stands the Priory Hall. This was built in 1848 as a National School on land given by the landowner and benefactor, Sir Watkyn Williams Wynn. Building costs were covered by funds raised through public subscription. The school closed in 1952 and thirty years later it became a community centre for the people of Wenlock. Another Victorian building houses the present Museum but was erected in 1878 as an open market hall. After the First World War it was rather unattractively extended to form a Memorial Hall. Many residents remember the important function it fulfilled later in the twentieth century as a cinema!

The Square, much changed as a result of rebuilding in the late 1980s, is now a public space used by locals and visitors alike. Criticised for imposing too genteel a face on what had been a vigorously utilitarian working area, it now offers a meeting-point or resting place and is a sun-trap in good weather. Its new look, incorporating the restored Jubilee clock, illustrates rather aptly Much Wenlock's transition from a working focus of rural business to its new role as a tourist attraction and desirable place to live.

Among the few twentieth century buildings of note, the largest residential property on Southfield Road, clearly visible from the Bridgnorth road, is now a nursing home. Formerly known as Corris House, it housed a Dr Barnardo's home for orphaned boys between

1930-1979. Many residents remember the boys walking to church every Sunday in an orderly crocodile down Barrow Street.

During the eighteenth century it was fashionable to re-face older properties with symmetrical brick facades and many of the houses along Wilmore and Barrow Streets are much older than they look, some incorporating Saxon elements. The Much Wenlock and District Society has provided historical notes to the town's shops and it is worth reading these. An antique shop on Barrow Street, for example, is recorded as a medieval hall with timber dating from the fourteenth century by tree-ring analysis.

Wenlock's four medieval almshouses were demolished and replaced by these in Sheinton Street in 1819. Still in use for elderly people, they are adorned with charming mock-Tudor arched doorways.

The Gaskell Arms is an old coaching inn, known in 1822 as the White Hart, where the Hibernia coach en route from Shrewsbury to Cheltenham, could change horses. In medieval times it was the site of Rindleford Hall, home of the Lawley family. In the fork between the Craven Arms and Church Stretton roads stand the imposing brick-built Old Rectory, dating from the early nineteenth century. Opposite, and sadly in a decayed condition at the time of writing, stands another house with clerical connections, Pinefield. Its large bow windows suggesting an eighteenth-century date, it was the home of D.H.S. Cranage, later to become Dean of Norwich, who wrote an early but still authoritative account of the churches of Shropshire whilst he was curate at Holy Trinity.

Many of Much Wenlock's buildings housed leather production operations. The top floor of the three-storey brick cottages, c.1840, in St Milburga's Row, was used as a drying out area for skins in the process of tanning. Known as Roushill, it was considered a slum area and given a wide berth by respectable folk. The process of tanning required large quantities of animal waste and the smells must have been overpowering!

Although the railway has long since been abandoned, various railway buildings can still be found, including the handsome station, now a private house, near the William Brookes School.

Travellers' Wenlock

Close to an area developed by the Romans, Much Wenlock was clearly a favoured spot, chosen as the site of the Anglo-Saxon Priory. Its importance, half way between his fortresses in Shrewsbury and Bridgnorth, was reinforced by the Norman Earl Roger when he re-endowed the monastic settlement even before establishing his own new abbey in Shrewsbury. It was part of a network of routes and communications between important strongholds, made even more accessible by the road to Bridgnorth over Harley Bank, constructed possibly by Henry III.

The Abbey, with its extensive landholdings, made the town into a commercial centre. The ancient layout which still persists today reflects Wenlock's status as a T-junction of converging roads, primitive though these were. It was not until Tudor times that any form of large-scale commercial haulage was in use but by the 1550s packhorses and wagons were travelling long distances to and from London. The first horse-drawn passenger coach in England is believed to have been introduced in 1555 and ten years later long four-wheeled goods waggons were in common use more or less everywhere, presupposing reasonable roads by the standards of the time.

By Tudor times, maintenance of roads was considered the responsibility of those who lived by them, and the Quarter Sessions monitored and enforced this duty. In many parts of rural Shropshire this was not unreasonable as local people were the principal road users. Busy roads, however, supporting the increasing commercial traffic from far afield, were another matter, and the setting up of Turnpike Trusts, established by Acts of Parliament, was a means of diverting the costs of maintenance to road users. The trusts were entitled to collect tolls, to buy land and to build and improve roads. The route from Bridgnorth to Shrewsbury was a turnpike road, its surface improved to facilitate fast driving (of horse-drawn wheeled vehicles) by the time the first mail coaches ran in 1785. Rapid delivery of mail, and the need for speedier personal travel, made it well worth paying a toll to the Turnpike Trust.

The Turnpike Trust marked distances with triangular cast-iron mileposts many of which can still be spotted. One important road, built in 1843 between Shipton and Morville, allowed commercial carriers to cut out the effort of traversing the Clee Hills. However, it was the last main road to be built in Shropshire before the railways transformed travel for ever.

But by the eighteenth century, Much Wenlock was a base for horse-drawn transport of all kinds. Every day a carrier left the Swan and Falcon public house (now Barclays Bank) with a delivery service of goods for the Corve Dale, and farmers and their wives drove waggons and pack-horses and rode to market themselves on solid, hardy Welsh cobs and donkeys.

The hey-day of coaching, vividly represented on so many nostalgic Christmas cards, was in fact a fairly brief couple of decades just prior to the coming of the railways. The first stage-coach to take passengers to London left Shrewsbury in 1753 and the journey took three and a half days. Twenty years later this time had been halved and, soon after Queen Victoria's accession in 1837, you could get to London in eighteen hours. Horses were generally changed after about ten miles and Much Wenlock was a staging post for this between Bridgnorth and Shrewsbury. Walking around Wenlock at that date you could hardly avoid the sight and smell of sweating horses, their grooms and waggons of hay and straw for their accommodation.

The advent of the railway in the early 1860s ushered in a period of increased prosperity for the town as it became possible for local limestone to reach more distant markets. Much Wenlock was among those Shropshire market towns which thrived in the nineteenth century because they were served by this new communication system.

The full panoply of the railway was brought here in 1861/2 by two separate business ventures, the Much Wenlock and Severn Junction Railway Company and the Much Wenlock Railway Company. For many years from the seventeenth century, a horse-operated railtrack, running down the Severn from the quarries of Wenlock Edge, had served industrial purposes. The steam locomotive, however, could transport local limestone far more quickly and easily to West Midlands ironworks or down river to those at Ironbridge. By 1864, passengers could travel from Much Wenlock to Hereford and Birmingham, connecting there with trains to London, a fact which greatly enhanced both the status and prosperity of the town.

For many generations before mass car-ownership the railway was a vital feature of Wenlock life. Pupils at the Coalbrookdale High School and employees of the Buildwas Power Station were among the numerous Wenlockians who used the train daily. Among many other users of this service were pigeon racers, who loaded baskets of birds onto the train for release at an arranged destination. Extra trains would always be laid on to serve the needs of visitors to the Wenlock Games.

All this local activity was sadly to change. By 1951 the railway was no longer available to passengers, although freight was still carried between Buildwas and Longville until 1963, when the line finally closed. This was a period when swingeing cuts in railway services were made all across Britain, a policy which now, in view of widespread concern over the environmental problems caused by the car, looks increasingly short-sighted.

By the end of the twentieth century, the construction of the M54 motorway had enabled Wenlock to attract commuters moving out from the urban centres of Wolverhampton and Birmingham. Local traffic, including agricultural, and industrial haulage from Telford, has become increasingly heavier but, at the time of writing, the hoped-for Wenlock by-pass has not materialised.

The Square today. (Penny-farthing)

Ahead

Much Wenlock, at the beginning of the twenty-first century, is a great deal busier and more prosperous than it was twenty years ago when there were empty shops on the High Street. In spite of the sharp decline in farming and the many problems consequent on that, there is more or less full employment, provided by agricultural businesses, and light industry here as well as in nearby Telford. Residual quarrying, and haulage associated with that, continue to provide work. In addition, and of increasing importance for the whole hinterland of Ironbridge, tourism now provides substantial employment.

As well as the appeal of the Edge for walkers and the increasing numbers of leisure horseriders, Much Wenlock is fortunate in possessing, in its monastic ruins, a major historic site maintained by English Heritage. Holy Trinity church is also much-visited and maintains a thriving congregation. The County Council runs a library and a small museum, open from the spring to autumn months. These attractions help to maintain a constant flow of visitors and a future for the various hotels, restaurants, cafes, gift, clothes and antique shops. A recent addition to the features of local interest is the Olympian Trail, inaugurated in 2000, which offers visitors more information about early Olympic history. The active civic society has ambitious plans to preserve and restore the Windmill, using the adjacent land with its varied habitats as a local amenity.

It is possible to live in Much Wenlock and do most of your shopping here; the town continues to provide basic services, with a Post Office, chemist, high quality butcher and several bakeries. It has a medical centre and a veterinary practice, although the one remaining blacksmith deals only with decorative work. At the hardware shop, which supplies everything for the DIY enthusiast, you can have dry-cleaning done. A number of artists and craftspeople have chosen to work here and there are three very different private gallery-shops as well as a pottery.

Much Wenlock's primary and secondary schools are well-supported and successful, the latter, founded in 1953, with a large catchment area and a flourishing sixth form. The town runs a lively two-week arts festival in June of alternate years and supports a successful Male Voice Choir. It appears to have a bright and secure future as a popular place to live, especially because of demographic changes bringing former urban dwellers to country towns.

However, one aspect of this social change is damaging to the traditional community. Young people can no longer afford the costs of housing which is sold to better-off professional families, who may not stay more than a few years, and to the retired. Whilst the town affords a high quality of life to these groups, it offers very little, culturally or socially, for the young and may risk becoming isolated from the mainstream of national life. In spite of government initiatives to discourage reliance on the car, public transport remains inadequate and unpopular. As with many other historic towns, traffic and parking in the central Conservation Area are problems as yet unresolved.

Further Reading

The Victoria County History, Vol X, Wenlock, Upper Corvedale and the Stretton Hills

Wenlock in the Middle Ages, W F Mumford

The Old Houses of Shropshire, C Forrest

Spring in a Shropshire Abbey, Lady C Milnes Gaskell

Old Shropshire Life, Lady C Milnes Gaskell

The Industrial Revolution in Shropshire, B Trinder

The Archaeology of the Welsh Marches, S C Stanford

Appendix

Place Names

The origins of the name Wenlock are uncertain. The land acquired by St Milburga was named Wimnicas but the closeness of the Welsh border suggests that the Welsh Gwyn-loc, or white monastery, might refer to the white walls of her sanctuary, which, like other important buildings of the time, was probably limewashed.

The suffix 'leah', found in a number of the outlying hamlets (Farley, Atterley, Harley, Hughley) is Anglo-Saxon, but not earlier than the middle of the eighth century It refers to a settlement in a woodland clearing and probably indicates the substantial woodland clearance which went on at that period. 'Tun' , which also indicates a settlement, as in Callaughton, Stretton and Sheinton, may be older.

The place-name element 'walh'- as in Walton, was used by the Anglo-Saxons to denote Celtic occupation, although it was also applied to settlements of serfs who may not have been of Celtic origin. Some local names indicate activities, as with Brick Yard near

Atterley, Brick Leasow near Bourton and Brickkiln Piece near
Presthope. The name Bourton incorporates the Anglo-Saxon 'burh'
used of a fortified settlement, while the element 'brock' as in
Brockton, denotes the presence of badgers at some time. Barrow is
a hill or burial mound and 'bold', as in Oxenbold, is a building.
The river Severn has a Celtic name; the 'h' in the Welsh 'hafren'
has been replaced with an 's'.

The Romans had surprisingly little influence on place names and even
their word for a military camp, 'castra', was applied to settlements
(as in Lancaster and Chester) not by them but by the Celts, who gave
the Roman town of Viroconium the name Wroxeter. The Normans
came as conquerors rather than as settlers of the countryside, and their
influence, too, is limited. The French 'ville' in Morville implies a
landowner's domain rather than a town. The term "vill" is used in
the Domesday Book to record a manor or estate.

Some names come from ancient folk tales such as those surrounding
the ghostly robber, Ippikin (see p1). His status is that of a sort of
hobgoblin, once probably a Celtic deity, demoted by Christianity and
his name is considered to derive from that of the ancient Celtic wood
spirit, Puck, celebrated so famously in Shakespeare's Midsummer
Night's Dream. Folk memories of Puck are to be found throughout
England and in this part of the world there are two place names
which probably recall him, Pickthorn, near Stottesdon, and
Powkesmoor, near Ditton Priors. This name (like Monkhopton) has
obvious monastic connections and Ditton itself means a farm or ditch.

Index

More books on Shropshire's history published by Shropshire Books

A MUCH WENLOCK TOWN TRAIL £1.00
WALKS AROUND MUCH WENLOCK £1.00
Both available from the TIC and bookshop

SHROPSHIRE IN THE CIVIL WAR £10.99
Terry Bracher and Roger Emmett

SHREWSBURY ABBEY: A MEDIEVAL MONASTERY . . £6.95
Nigel Baker

MEDIEVAL SHREWSBURY £7.95
Dorothy Cromarty

TUDOR SHREWSBURY £7.95
Bill Champion

SHROPSHIRE FROM THE AIR:
MAN AND THE LANDSCAPE £13.99
Michael Watson and Chris Musson

SHROPSHIRE FROM THE AIR:
AN ENGLISH COUNTY AT WORK £12.99
Michael Watson and Chris Musson

For a complete list of all our books and leaflets on Shropshire please contact:

Shropshire Books
The Annexe
Shirehall
Abbey Foregate
SHREWSBURY
SY2 6ND
Telephone: 01743 255043
Fax: 01743 255050
or visit our website at:
www.shropshirebooks.co.uk